The **MARMITE** Cookbook

The **MARMITE** Cookbook
Paul Hartley

Absolute Press

In association with
www.breakfastandbrunch.com.

First published in Great Britain in 2003
by **Absolute Press**
Scarborough House
29 James Street West
Bath BA1 2BT
Phone 44 (0) 1225 316013
Fax 44 (0) 1225 445836
E-mail info@absolutepress.co.uk
Website www.absolutepress.co.uk
Reprinted 2003 (twice), 2004

© Paul Hartley, 2003
© Absolute Press, 2003

ISBN 1 904573 09 6

Printed and bound by
Printer Trento, Italy

Araldite®, Bovril®, Philadelphia®,
Tabasco Sauce®, and Walkers®
are all registered trademarks.

Marmite® is a registered trademark.
All Marmite copyright material and
registered trademarks are reproduced
with the permission of the Unilever
Group of Companies.

Any information contained within
this book has been based upon
the research and the opinions of the
author and publisher. This information
does not represent the opinions of the
Unilever Group of Companies.

Contents

Growing-up spread...

Great on toast...

Store-cupboard essential...

Great British icon...

Love it, hate it...

'Yuck.'
Carol Smilie, TV presenter

'Love it.'
Colin Dexter, author

'My husband has some in
the cupboard, but I'm not sure
what it is...'
Nicole Fahri, fashion designer

'Marmite? I love it. I started
eating it later in life when I was
recording commercials. All the
young people I was working with
would have it for breakfast which
was very sweet. I like Bovril, too.'
Tom Baker, actor

'What is Marmite? [Interviewer
explains....] I've never had it.
I'd love to try it. Perhaps you
could you send me some?'
Gerard Depardieu, actor

'Hate it.'
Jackie Collins, novelist

but don't take our word for it.

Marmite

Recipe

Collection

Seared Beef and Beansprout Wrap

LOVE

MARIE E. VILMOT
Hamburg, Germany

'The yummiest thing ever
to come out of the UK.'

1 Firstly put two plates in the oven to warm. Put the beef and the red pepper into a bowl. Add the sesame oil and Marmite and mix all together roughly so that the meat and the pepper become well coated.

2 Heat a wok or frying pan to a high heat and add the mixture, cooking quite quickly to sear the ingredients and to just cook the beef. At this point add 2 handfuls of beansprouts and toss it all together for 2 minutes.

3 Place a Chinese pancake on each warmed plate and then pile on the steak, beansprouts and peppers. Wrap up the pancake and devour immediately.

SERVES 2

150g rump steak, thinly sliced
1/2 red pepper, cut into strips
1 tablespoon sesame oil
1 teaspoon Marmite
1 pack beansprouts
2 Chinese pancake wraps

Pasta Primavera

SERVES 2

50g broad beans, fresh or frozen
50g unsalted butter
50g green beans
75g mangetout
200g pasta ribbons
  (fettuccine or tagliatelle)
1 heaped teaspoon Marmite
1 tablespoon chopped
  fresh chives
1 tablespoon chopped
  flatleaf parsley
Black pepper

1 Cook the broad beans in a little boiling water for about 2-3 minutes (slightly longer if frozen), drain them and pop them out of their shells with your thumb and finger. Put them into a medium-sized saucepan with the butter and keep to one side. Cook the green beans in boiling water for 3-4 minutes, adding the mangetout to cook for the last minute. Then drain and add them to the broad beans. Don't compromise the sweet taste of the vegetables by adding salt when you cook them.

2 Cook the pasta in boiling water for about 10 minutes until just tender. Drain, leaving a little moisture on the pasta, return it to the hot pan and add the Marmite and stir until the pasta is well coated. Now add the warm vegetables and chopped herbs to the pasta and give the whole mixture a gentle stir over a very low heat, seasoning with plenty of freshly ground black pepper. Serve on hot plates and enjoy the wonderful fresh flavours.

Peach, Parma Ham and Ricotta Sandwich

SERVES 4

4 small ciabatta breads
1 teaspoon Marmite
250g ricotta
4 large slices Parma ham
2 ripe peaches, stoned and sliced
Handful of salad leaves
Fresh black pepper

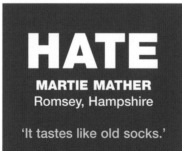

HATE

MARTIE MATHER
Romsey, Hampshire

'It tastes like old socks.'

1 Halve the 4 ciabatta breads and open them up. Mix together the Marmite and ricotta cheese and spread liberally inside each ciabatta.

2 Divide the Parma ham, peaches and salad leaves equally between the 4 breads, and season with fresh pepper. Replace the top of the sandwich and enjoy.

Savoury Waffles with Pumpkin and Pancetta

MAKES 8 WAFFLES

200g pumpkin or butternut squash,
   peeled, deseeded and diced
100g cubed pancetta
A drizzle of olive oil
180g plain flour
120g fine cornmeal
2 teaspoons baking powder
2 eggs, separated
225ml milk
200ml natural yoghurt
1 teaspoon Marmite
Maple syrup
Freshly ground pepper

1 Mix together the pumpkin or butternut squash and pancetta, drizzle with a little olive oil and roast in a medium-hot oven (375°F/190°C/Gas 6) for 20 minutes.

2 To make the waffles; sift the flour, cornmeal and baking powder into a large bowl. Put the egg yolks into another bowl, add the milk, yoghurt, Marmite and 2 tablespoons of olive oil and whisk well. Add the flour mixture and beat well. Put the egg whites into a clean bowl and whisk until you have stiff peaks. Then using a large metal spoon gently fold the egg whites into the waffle batter.

3 Depending on the size of your waffle maker, spoon about 125ml of the batter into a heated and lightly oiled waffle iron, or follow the instructions of your waffle maker. Cook until crisp – about 4-5 minutes, keep warm and repeat until all the batter is used. Place a waffle on each plate and using a slotted spoon pile the roasted pumpkin or butternut squash and pancetta on top, drizzled with lashings of maple syrup. Serve immediately.

You will need an electric waffle iron or waffle maker for this recipe.

Crispy Roasted Fennel and New Potato Salad

1 Boil the new potatoes in salted water for 15-20 minutes until cooked through. Drain and keep warm.

2 Take the pack of Marmite crisps, make a small hole at one end of the packet to let the air escape, and crush the contents with a rolling pin. Empty the contents onto a plate. Cut each fennel bulb into about 8 large wedges and brush each cut side with olive oil. Then plunge the oiled sides into the crushed crisps to coat them. Sprinkle a hint of olive oil on a roasting tin and place the fennel wedges, uncoated side down, in the tin and roast in a hot oven (430°F/220°C/Gas 8) for 15 minutes. The fennel should be softened and the coating crispy.

3 Take 4 serving plates and strew each with the dressed mixed leaves. Then add the new potatoes and fennel wedges and season with salt and plenty of fresh black pepper.

SERVES 4

16 baby new potatoes
Salt and black pepper
1 pack Walkers Marmite crisps
2 large fennel bulbs
A drizzle of olive oil
Dressed mixed salad leaves

VEGGIES LOVE IT TOO

In traditional beermaking a gelatin-like subject called isinglass (obtained from fish such as sturgeon) is used to clear cloudy particles from the brew. But this process takes place *after* the yeast extract has been removed, thus making Marmite a bona fide 100% veggie spread!

Griddled Haddock Jacket with Marmite Cheese Sauce

SERVES 2

2 medium baking potatoes
A little olive oil
Coarse sea salt
25ml milk
1 teaspoon Marmite
100g Emmental cheese, grated
Freshly milled black and white
    pepper (black for flavour, white
    for strength)
150g natural smoked
    haddock fillets
Fresh chopped parsley

1 Scrub the potatoes and coat with olive oil and a sprinkling of coarse sea salt – best to use your hands for this. A good tip is to bake the spuds on a metal kebab skewer; they will cook quicker and more evenly. Bake the spuds in the oven 425°F/210°C/Gas 7 for 45 minutes.

2 About ten minutes before the potatoes have baked, warm the milk gently in a small saucepan adding the Marmite. Fold in the grated Emmental stirring gently until the cheese is coated and only just beginning to melt. Season with a good grind of pepper – just imagine how delicious this is going to be on the potato, and remove from the heat.

3 Brush a griddle with a little olive oil and when hot, sear the skinned haddock for 3 minutes on each side to seal in the flavour.

4 Cut each hot jacket potato with a cross and pressing from the sides, open them up, cut the fish into chunks and spoon into the potato, then spoon over the Marmite cheesy mixture. Now pop it under a hot grill for a couple of minutes until the cheese starts to drizzle. Finally sprinkle this scrummy dish with lots of roughly chopped parsley – all the flavours will fuse together.

Morning Mushrooms

1 Pre-heat the grill to medium. Wipe the mushrooms clean with a damp cloth and trim the stalks down to the gills. Brush the mushrooms, gill side up, with olive oil and season with pepper. Place side by side in a baking dish and cook under the grill for 3-4 minutes.

2 Cook the spinach in a microwave or a saucepan with a small amount of water until wilted. Drain. Remove the mushrooms from the grill and turn the heat up to high. Drain the spinach thoroughly, mix in the Marmite and divide into four. Place each spinach portion firmly onto a mushroom, then top each spinach mound first with grated Gruyère and then with Parmesan.

Return the stacks to the grill and cook until the cheese begins to melt down over the spinach and mushrooms.

3 Place two stacks on each serving plate, sprinkle with toasted pine kernels and some thyme leaves and serve immediately with toasted focaccia or granary wedges.

SERVES 2

4 flat field mushrooms
A little olive oil
Sea salt and ground black pepper
150g fresh spinach
1 teaspoon Marmite
50g freshly grated Gruyère cheese
25g freshly grated Parmesan cheese
2 tablespoons toasted pine kernels
Fresh thyme leaves
 (or a pinch of dried thyme)
Toasted focaccia or granary wedges, to serve

MARMITE SHRINE

Contrary to popular belief, Marmite does have its fans in the US. Its chief flag bearer is possibly Missouri-based Doug Schneider, who established his very own shrine to the yellow-lidded stuff in the form of the Missouri Marmite Museum.

Roasted Onions with Marmite Sausages

1 Bring a large pan of water to the boil and cook the whole and unpeeled onions, for 15-20 minutes. Drain the onions and allow them to cool until easy to handle.

2 Put the prunes, sausagemeat, Marmite, rosemary and black pepper into a bowl and mash thoroughly – using the back of a spoon is an easy way to do this.

3 Pre-heat the oven to 200°C/400°F/Gas 6. Cut off the lid of each onion and scoop out the middle third of each onion with a teaspoon – you can always use this for a soup – and fill the hole with the sausage mixture. Drizzle with the olive oil and roast in the oven for 30-35 minutes. Great served with a leafy salad and some good crusty bread.

SERVES 4

8 medium onions
50g dried prunes, stoned and finely chopped
350g good quality sausagemeat
2 teaspoons Marmite
1 level teaspoon chopped rosemary
Fresh black pepper
1 tablespoon olive oil
25g unsalted butter

Doug's collection started humbly enough, way back in 1973, when he was living in the UK. He held onto the 'adorable' metal-capped jar, keen to retain this memento that struck him as so very British. Doug's travels took him to many countries, and he began to pick up more Marmite jars – from Canada, Sri Lanka and Hong Kong to name a few. That's when the collecting bug really started to drive him: he dug up an antique jar from a Welsh trash heap; he located tins that used to house Marmite stock cubes, and, of course, he discovered the internet and a worldwide homage – hundreds of Marmite items, from the bespoke to the mass-produced to the outright weird (Marmite candle, anyone?). The museum is located in Valley Park and, via prior arrangement with Doug, is open to the public. A Marmite-sweatshirted Doug surveys a few items from his collection (left).

Naandwich (Chilli Scramble in Indian Bread)

SERVES 2

4 large free-range eggs
1 fresh green chilli, finely diced
1 tablespoon chopped sun-dried
  tomatoes
1 level dessertspoon Parmesan,
2-3 drops Tabasco Sauce
Freshly milled black and white
  pepper (black for aroma and
  flavour, white for heat)
2 mini naan breads
  (from supermarkets)
25g unsalted butter
Marmite for spreading
Freshly chopped coriander leaves

This is scrambled egg with a kick. If you prefer a milder heat reduce the quantities of chilli and Tabasco Sauce according to your taste.

1 In a bowl break the eggs and add the chilli, sun-dried tomatoes, Parmesan, 2-3 drops of Tabasco Sauce and a good grind of pepper. Whisk not only to mix the ingredients but also to add air, which will make it light and fluffy.

2 Take the round Naan bread and slice off one edge to form a pocket, pop the naan breads in a toaster cut end down. This will make them easy to open once warmed.

3 In a non-stick pan melt the butter on a medium heat and when hot add the egg mixture. This will cook very quickly - you are looking for a 'just-set' consistency. Cook it too little and it will be runny, cook it too much and it will be bouncy. It is important to use a wooden spoon and to keep stirring all the time.

4 Spread the inside of the warm naan breads with Marmite (as little or as much as you like – but remember both the Marmite and the sun-dried tomatoes will add a salty taste). Spoon in the delicious and fluffy chilli scramble, sprinkle with fresh coriander and serve immediately.

Indubitably for people of good taste. And certainly more than just a sandwich filler.

Boston Baked Beans

SERVES 10

1kg dried haricot beans,
  soaked overnight
100ml molasses or black treacle
2 tablespoons brown sugar
2 teaspoons dry mustard
  powder
2 teaspoons Marmite
1 teaspoon ground black pepper
1 medium sized onion, peeled
500g belly of pork with rind

1 Cover the soaked beans with fresh water and bring to the boil skimming off any foam. Reduce the heat and simmer the beans until their skins begin to burst. Drain the beans and reserve the cooking liquid. Combine the molasses, brown sugar, mustard powder, Marmite and pepper with the cooking liquid.

2 Heat the oven to 100°C/ 200°F/Gas lowest. Place the onion in the bottom of a 2-litre ovenproof casserole and pour the beans on the top. Score the rind of the pork and push it down into the beans rind side up. Pour the seasoned liquid on top adding enough boiling water to cover the beans. Cover the casserole and bake in the oven for a mere nine hours!

3 Every hour add boiling water, if necessary, to keep the beans covered. Remove the cover for the last hour of baking so that the pork browns. Serve with the pork on top of the beans and accompany with chunks of the best sourdough bread available.

Spicy Sausage, Parsley and Caper Salad with Marmite Vinaigrette

SERVES 2

4 spicy sausages
   (merguez or similar)
1/2 small red onion,
   peeled and thinly sliced
1 tablespoon capers, rinsed
2 handfuls flat leaf parsley,
   chopped
Freshly ground black pepper
1 freshly baked baguette,
   cut in half lengthways

FOR THE VINAIGRETTE
45ml olive oil
20ml white wine vinegar
1/2 teaspoon Dijon mustard
2 freshly chopped basil leaves
1/2 teaspoon runny honey
1 level teaspoon Marmite

1 To prepare the Marmite vinaigrette simply whizz together all the vinaigrette ingredients for about 30 seconds, until it emulsifies. This Marmite vinaigrette is great for all sorts of salads and can be kept in the fridge for 2-3 days.

2 Grill or fry the sausages until cooked, then slice thickly and keep them warm. Mix together the onion, capers and parsley. Combine the cooked sausage with the parsley salad and toss in the Marmite vinaigrette. Toast the cut side of the baguettes and pile the sausage salad mixture onto each half. Serve while still warm, seasoned with black pepper.

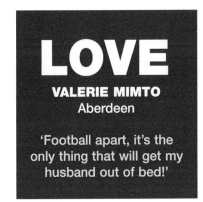

Deep-fried Eggs with Tomato Sauce

SERVES 4

Oil for deep-frying
4 large free-range eggs
4 slices rustic bread
Marmite for spreading
Ground black pepper
Pinch cumin seeds
Salt

FOR THE TOMATO SAUCE

30ml olive oil
1/2 onion, chopped
1 clove garlic, chopped
400g tin of Italian chopped
  tomatoes
1 tablespoon of tomato puree
Pinch cayenne pepper
Squeeze lemon juice
Salt
Ground black pepper
1/2 teaspoon dried oregano
1 teaspoon caster sugar

1 First make the tomato sauce. Heat half the olive oil in a saucepan and sauté the chopped onion and garlic until soft. Add the tin of chopped tomatoes, and tomato purée and simmer for 20-25 minutes to reduce the sauce and create a deeper flavour. Add the cayenne, lemon juice, salt and pepper and blend until smooth. Stir in the oregano and the remaining olive oil and leave to one side.

2 Heat the frying oil until a cube of bread becomes brown and crisp in 60 seconds. Deep-fry the eggs one at a time: break each egg into an oiled ladle and lower the ladle into the hot oil.

As the oil begins to bubble around the egg, remove the ladle. Using a slotted spoon, gently roll the egg over once or twice to enfold the yolk in the white. Cook for 50-55 seconds until the white is fluffy and golden and the yolk still soft. Remove the egg, drain on kitchen paper and keep warm in a low oven while cooking the remaining eggs.

3 Toast the bread and spread with Marmite. Re-heat the tomato sauce and place each egg on a slice of Marmite toast on a warmed plate. Season with salt, pepper and cumin. Cover each egg with 2-3 tablespoons of the tomato sauce and serve immediately.

Marmite breath...
not the most romantic
Valentine's Day wake-up call!
But then there are those who
would disagree, of course....

Tuna and Sweetcorn Pancakes

MAKES 6-8 PANCAKES

FOR THE PANCAKES
1 egg
1 teaspoon Marmite
300ml milk
25g plain flour
Vegetable oil

FOR THE FILLING AND TOPPING
A small knob of butter
1 small tin sweetcorn, drained
2 tablespoons crème fraîche
1 small tin tuna
50g grated Emmental
Handful of cashews
Handful of crisps

1 First make the pancakes by whisking the egg, Marmite and milk together and then gradually blending in the flour until you have a smooth batter mixture. Leave to stand for 10 minutes.

2 Heat a lightly oiled non-stick frying pan and spoon a tablespoon of batter mixture into the pan. Swirl the batter around to coat the base of the pan and as soon as bubbles appear in the batter flip the pancake over. Repeat with the remaining mixture, keeping the cooked pancakes warm in a low oven.

3 In a saucepan melt the butter and over a gentle heat add the sweetcorn, followed by the crème fraîche and then the tuna. Turn the mixture gently to warm through. Take one pancake and spoon $\frac{1}{6}$ of the tuna mixture down the centre and roll it up. Follow with the other 5 pancakes and put them side-by-side in an ovenproof dish. Sprinkle with the grated cheese and pop the dish under a hot grill for a couple of minutes to melt the cheese. Serve the warm pancakes scattered with crushed crisps and chopped cashew nuts.

Banana and Bacon French Toast

SERVES 1

2 rashers unsmoked back bacon
2 slices rustic stale white bread
Marmite for spreading
1 banana, peeled and mashed
Pinch of cinnamon
1 medium free-range egg
25ml milk
25g unsalted butter

1 Grill the bacon until just crispy. Spread one slice of bread with Marmite and then the mashed banana, a sprinkling of cinnamon and top with the rashers of crispy bacon. Put the other slice of bread onto the sandwich and press down firmly.

2 In a flat dish whisk together the egg and milk and dip both sides of the sandwich into it. Meanwhile melt the butter in a heavy based frying pan until just sizzling, then add the French toast sandwich. Cook for a few minutes on each side until golden and crispy. Devour while still warm.

HATE

TIM RATHMEARE
Hove, Sussex

'I use it for fish bait, but there's no place for it outside my tackle box.'

Chicken, Avocado and Marmite Mayo Wrap

SERVES 2

1 breast of chicken
1 teaspoon Marmite
1 small green chilli
4 rashers good streaky bacon
2 flour tortilla wraps
2 tablespoons 'lite' mayonnaise
1 avocado, peeled and stoned
Black pepper
Juice of ½ lime

1 Coat the chicken breast with Marmite and sprinkle over the finely chopped green chilli. Wrap it loosely in kitchen foil and bake in a medium oven 350°F/180°C /Gas 5 for about 30 minutes. When the chicken is almost ready grill the bacon until crispy. Gently warm the tortilla on a hot dry griddle or in the oven for 2-3 minutes.

2 Lay out the tortilla and spread the whole of it with mayonnaise. Slice the chicken breast and divide between the 2 tortillas. Crumble the crispy bacon on the top and finally add slices of avocado. Season generously with freshly milled black pepper and a sprinkle of fresh lime juice to really bring the flavours alive.

3 Now fold up the bottom half of the wrap, fold in the 2 sides and hold in place with a napkin. Serve with a bottle of ice-cold Mexican beer.

When assembling this tortilla, imagine what it's going to look like when it's finished and remember all the ingredients are going to be wrapped, so place them away from the 'bottom' of the tortillas.

Marmite Garlic Bread

SERVES 4

2 cloves garlic,
    peeled and crushed
1 teaspoon Marmite
1 teaspoon dried mixed herbs
125g unsalted butter, softened
1 French stick

1 Pre-heat the oven to medium-high 375°F/190°C/Gas 6. Into a bowl add the garlic, Marmite and mixed herbs to the softened butter and mash the whole lot together with a fork.

2 Cut the French stick on the bias at 2-3cm intervals, without cutting all the way through. Spread plenty of the garlic butter into each cut slice of bread and then wrap the whole French stick in kitchen foil. Place on a baking tray and cook in the oven for about 20 minutes.

3 Carefully open the foil, leaving the top of the French stick exposed and return it to the oven for 5 more minutes to crisp the top of the bread.

4 To serve, place the board in the centre of the table and rip off chunks of crispy hot garlic bread. I bet there won't be any left over!

TAT-TOO GOOD

When granting first-time tattooist and life-long friend Kev Smith free reign with inks upon his arm, Russell Tuck, from Ulverstone in Cumbria, could think of no more fitting an image than a jar of his beloved Marmite. Russell was chuffed with the result and his love for the spread is undiminished. Kev still sports a photo of Russell's arm in his tattoo shop window.

Staffordshire Oatcakes with Goat's Cheese, Spinach and Walnuts

SERVES 2

100g frozen spinach, defrosted
1 teaspoon Marmite
1 pack Staffordshire oatcakes
(This is a pancake-like product
available from supermarkets)
100g soft goat's cheese
25g chopped walnuts
2 teaspoons snipped chives
Freshly milled black pepper

1 Warm the spinach gently in a pan, adding a dash of water if needed, and then beat in the Marmite and cook gently for a couple of minutes. You can as an alternative mix the 2 together and heat in a microwave. Keep the mixture warm while you heat the oatcakes in a low oven, 325°F/170°C/Gas 4.

2 When they are warm divide the goat's cheese between the 2 oatcakes and spread it right over. Drain the warm spinach thoroughly and then scatter it over the goat's cheese. Next strew the chopped walnuts over the spinach and season with fresh black pepper.

3 Roll up each oatcake and top with the snipped chives to garnish. For extra fun you can secure each roll with a cocktail stick, cut them in half at an angle and stand them up like chimneys.

LOVE
RAVI E. MOLMETI
Blackburn, Lancashire

'After the last scrape, I fill the jar with warm water and drink out the dregs.'

Grange Asparagus Brunch

1 Steam the fresh asparagus until its cooked but still has a crunch. Keep warm. Brush the tomatoes and button mushrooms with olive oil and pop them under a medium grill for about 4 minutes. Do not over cook them or the tomato skins will split and the mushrooms will become crispy.

2 Toast the bread and then spread it with Marmite according to your taste. Place the asparagus on the toast, 2 pieces horizontally and 2 vertically with equal gaps to form a 'chequer-board'.

3 Place a tomato in the top right hand corner, the central square and the bottom left hand corner, fill the remaining gaps with the button mushrooms and before devouring you can play noughts and crosses!

SERVES 1

4 stems fresh asparagus
3 cherry tomatoes
6 button mushrooms
A little olive oil
1 slice of good country bread
Marmite for spreading

This dish was influenced by Sarah from the Whatley Grange Cookery School, Somerset.

Croustades of Seared Salmon and Tarragon Mayonnaise

FOR A FEW FRIENDS

2 tablespoons mayonnaise
Sprig of tarragon, finely chopped
1 teaspoon Marmite
1 small French stick
250g fresh salmon fillet
Olive oil for brushing
Handful rocket leaves
4 cherry tomatoes
Black pepper

1 Mix together the mayonnaise, tarragon and Marmite in a small bowl and set aside. Slice the French bread into rounds about 1cm thick and lightly toast on both sides. Take the salmon and cut into thin slices a little smaller than the toast rounds they are going to nestle on. Brush each side of the salmon with a little olive oil and sear on a griddle for a couple of minutes.

2 Take the toasted breads and spread each with a teaspoon of the Marmite mayo then lay a piece of salmon on each. Top the salmon with a couple of rocket leaves, slices of cherry tomatoes and a good flourish of fresh black pepper. Lovely eaten warm but also delicious cold.

TAXI!

The livery of the London cab received a facelift during 2002, Marmite's centenary year. Thirty-three of them were decked out in distinctive eye-catching split-personality uniforms, with one side proclaiming '100 years of love', the other '100 years of hate'.

Quails' Eggs and Bockwurst Salad with Marmite Dressing

1 Boil the baby new potatoes in salted water for about 15 minutes. Meanwhile gently grill the Bockwurst until cooked. Boil the quails' eggs for about 3 minutes. Plunge the eggs straight into cold water just until you can handle them and then remove the shells.

2 Make the salad dressing by placing all the ingredients into a blender and blitzing for about 30-50 seconds until they have emulsified.

3 Drain the new potatoes and allow them to cool a little. In a large bowl put the salad leaves, new potatoes and Bockwurst cut into thin slices on the diagonal. Add the dressing and toss them all very gently.

4 Place the coated leaves, Bockwurst and potatoes onto 2 plates then top with halved quails eggs. Season with a good grind of black pepper and enjoy while still warm with fresh crusty bread.

SERVES 2

8 baby new potatoes
2 Bockwurst sausages
6 quails' eggs
Cos or little gem lettuce leaves, roughly chopped

FOR THE SALAD DRESSING

45ml olive oil
1 level teaspoon Marmite
$1/2$ teaspoon Dijon mustard
25ml white wine vinegar
$1/2$ teaspoon runny honey
2 fresh basil leaves

Leftover dressing will keep in the refrigerator for 2-3 days.

Indonesian Brunch

SERVES 4

Groundnut oil for frying
6 shallots sliced lengthways
1 stick lemon grass,
   split open and finely diced
4oz peeled prawns
1 tablespoon fish sauce
3 mild red chillies, de-seeded
   and chopped
1 tablespoon sweet chilli sauce
1 teaspoon Marmite
100g button mushrooms
100g Shiitake mushrooms
250g long grain rice,
   cooked and cooled
4 medium free-range eggs

1 Heat two tablespoons of oil in a wok and fry the shallots, lemon grass and prawns for one minute. Then add the fish sauce and chilli and fry for a further 30 seconds. Next add the sweet chilli sauce and Marmite and toss together for 30 seconds. Finally add the mushrooms and the rice and stir-fry for about three minutes until it reaches a good deep colour.

2 Meanwhile fry the eggs keeping the yolks soft. Divide the rice mixture between warmed serving bowls. Top with a fried egg and accompany with a little informed and entertaining Oriental gossip.

HATE

EMMA HARRIETT
Dublin, Ireland
'I've eaten some unimaginable things... flies, locusts and worse. I draw the line at Marmite.'

Pork Burgers with Fresh Salsa

MAKES 6 BURGERS

450g finely minced belly of pork
1 small onion, finely chopped
1 teaspoon chopped sage
½ teaspoon grated nutmeg
1 teaspoon Marmite

FOR THE SALSA

1 medium red onion, finely diced
5 tomatoes, skinned, seeded
   and diced
1 red chilli, seeded and finely
   chopped
1 teaspoon sugar
Juice of 1 lime
2 tablespoons chopped fresh
   coriander leaves

1 Dunk the tomatoes in boiling water for 30 seconds to split their skins for easy removal.

2 Mix together all the salsa ingredients, add a pinch of salt and set aside. In a bowl mix together the minced pork, onion, sage, nutmeg and Marmite. Although it is a bit messy hands are definitely best for this. When all the ingredients are well combined, wet your hands and divide the mixture into 6 burgers. The water will prevent the mixture sticking to you. Put the burgers on greaseproof paper and chill for about 10 minutes to help them to set.

3 When ready, heat a lightly greased griddle and cook the burgers for 3-4 minutes on each side until they are thoroughly cooked through. Serve the hot burgers with the cool salsa for a mouth-watering combo.

Baked Eggs with Marmite Mushrooms

SERVES 4

25g butter
2 shallots,
 peeled and finely chopped
300g flat mushrooms finely
 chopped (keeping a few
 slices for garnish)
1/4 of a whole nutmeg grated
2 teaspoons Marmite
Freshly ground black pepper
3 tablespoons of créme
 fraîche or Greek yoghurt
4 large free-range eggs
Bunch of watercress

You will need 4 ramekins and a shallow roasting tin. This dish looks really impressive when you dunk your toasted soldiers into the golden yolk.

1 Heat half the butter in a small saucepan until it begins to sizzle. Add the shallots and cook on a low heat for five minutes until they have become transparent. Add the mushrooms, the nutmeg (warning – nutmeg is an aphrodisiac!), the remaining butter and the Marmite and season well with fresh pepper. Turn the heat right down and cook gently for a further 5-8 minutes until you have a lovely dark mixture.

2 Pre-heat the oven to 180°C/ 350°F/Gas 4. Stir one tablespoon of the créme fraîche or yoghurt into the mushrooms, then divide the mixture between the ramekins. Make an indentation, break an egg into each one and season. Stir the rest of the créme fraîche or yoghurt to loosen it, divide it between the dishes and spread gently over the egg using the back of a spoon.

3 Put a slice of mushroom on the top of each ramekin and stand the ramekins in the roasting tin with 2/3 cm of boiling water. Bake for 15-18 minutes. Serve with wholemeal toasted soldiers for dunking and garnish the plates with fresh watercress.

Roquefort, Prawn and Pear Salad

SERVES 4

100ml olive oil
55ml lemon juice
1 teaspoon Marmite
Freshly milled black pepper
Pinch smoked paprika
4 ripe pears
Mixed salad leaves
225g peeled prawns
100g Roquefort cheese
4 spring onions, diced

1 Put in a blender the olive oil and lemon juice, add the Marmite, pepper and smoked paprika and zap for 20-30 seconds.

2 Peel and core the pears and cut into 1cm slices and marinate in water and lemon juice to keep them from browning. (Lemon juice on its own will taint the natural flavour of the fruit).

3 On a plate, arrange a handful of mixed leaves into a nest. Lay in the sliced pear then the prawns and crumble the Roquefort over the top. Sprinkle on the spring onions and drizzle with the Marmite vinaigrette and serve.

NOT TO BE CONFUSED WITH...

Margate
A seaside town on the south-east heel of England.
Marmoset
A small tropical American monkey with a long tail and a silky coat.
Araldite®
A brand of adhesives of fantastic use to people who like to glue things together. *Kitchen spread feasibility tests advised against (could possibly cement knife to bread).*

Lamb Kofte and Crispy Cabbage

SERVES 4

FOR THE KOFTE

450g minced lamb
1 teaspoon Marmite
1 teaspoon ground cumin seeds
  (dry fried or roasted first)
2 tablespoons of chopped fresh
  coriander
1/2 teaspoon garam masala
1/2 teaspoon cayenne pepper
3 tablespoons plain yoghurt
2 eggs, beaten

FOR THE CRISPY CABBAGE

1 small white cabbage,
  shredded
  (as you would for coleslaw)
2 pickled dill cucumbers, thinly
  sliced
1 medium red chilli, finely diced
Black pepper, freshly ground
White pepper, freshly ground
Olive oil
Lime juice

1 Put all the Kofte ingredients, except the beaten egg, into a large bowl and mix thoroughly with your hands dipping your hands in water to avoid the mixture sticking to you, then shape into 20-24 equal-sized meatballs. Put the meatballs on greaseproof paper in the fridge for 20 minutes to set.

2 Mix the white cabbage, dill cucumber and red chilli in a salad bowl, season with freshly ground black and white pepper and dress with a little olive oil and lime juice.

3 Brush the Kofte with beaten egg and deep fry in small batches. Serve while still warm on the bed of crispy cabbage.

CARRYING THE TORCH

Marmite sponsored the 1956 British Olympic team. The Games of this twenty-sixth Olympiad were held in Melbourne, Australia, except for the equestrian events, which, due to Australia's strict six-month quarantine regulations, were switched, late, and at some inconvenience, to Stockholm in Sweden. This was (and

Tuscan Picnic Loaf

SERVES 6

1 Ciabatta loaf
250g sun-dried tomatoes,
  roughly chopped
250g mixed peppers in oil
1 dessertspoon Marmite
2 dessertspoons red pesto
100g pastrami
2 Italian plum tomatoes, sliced
100g Mozzarella, sliced
Handful fresh basil leaves
Freshly ground black pepper

1 Cut the ciabatta in half lengthways and remove a little of the soft bread in the centre to make way for the filling. Drizzle a tablespoon of oil from the sun-dried tomatoes and peppers over one half of the ciabatta and then spread the Marmite. Over the other half spread the red pesto.

2 Taking the base of the loaf layer the sun-dried tomatoes and then the peppers, then the pastrami. Pile the tomatoes and the Mozzarella on top and finish with a dozen fresh basil leaves and some freshly ground black pepper. Replace the lid of the loaf and press down firmly.

3 You can now slice the loaf into portions and enjoy, or wrap in greaseproof paper and pack in the picnic hamper. This loaf is perfect made the night before, kept in the fridge and sliced off for all the family to enjoy for lunch.

remains) the only occasion that events of the same Olympics had been held in different countries. Great Britain managed to bag a haul of 24 medals, six of them gold. Part of the legacy of the Melbourne Games was that it firmly established television sets in the homes and hearts of the Australian people.

Prior to the Games, there had been a widely-held perception that television was American and 'cheap'. Every Aussie wanted to watch the Games, though, and this made ownership of televisions respectable and popular, resulting in rocketing sales of television sets for the duration of the Olympics.

Pizza Milano de Chiviso

SERVES 2

1 pre-made pizza base
1 teaspoon Marmite
2 dessertspoons tomato purée
4 chestnut mushrooms, sliced
2 Italian plum tomatoes, sliced
2 slices (1cm thick) Milano
  salami, diced into cubes
8-10 separated rings of red
  onion
50g grated Mozzarella
1 teaspoon fresh chopped
  oregano (or a good pinch
  of dried)
Freshly ground black pepper
Olive oil

1 Pre-heat the oven to medium hot 375°F/190°C/ Gas 6. Spread the pizza base with Marmite and then the tomato purée. Next fan the mushroom slices followed by the tomato slices over the whole pizza. Top this with scattered salami cubes and the red onion rings and finally a flourish of grated Mozzarella.

2 Season with oregano, fresh black pepper and drizzle with a little olive oil. Cook in the oven for 10-15 minutes or until the pizza is cooked through. Serve with a glass of chilled Pinot Grigio.

Marmite and Watercress Toasted Soldiers

SERVES 2

1 teaspoon Marmite
4 medium slices of white bread
100g fresh watercress

No seasoning is required for this dish as the watercress is peppery and the Marmite salty.

1 Pre-heat the grill to hot. Spread a thin coating of Marmite over two of the bread slices and cover them with watercress. Lightly butter the other 2 slices and place on top of the watercress press them together firmly to make a sandwich. Trim off the crusts and toast until just golden on both sides.

2 Now cut them in half and each half again into 'soldiers'. Great to dip into large boiled chickens' eggs (superb with ducks' eggs) or excellent with soup or just on their own.o

POWERING ROCKET MAN

'I always take Marmite with me...'. So says Elton John of one of the 'stock essentials' he just can't do without whilst away on tour. In 1979, so the story goes, Elton played a series of concerts in Moscow and Leningrad, in the former Soviet Union. During the tour, Elton developed a hankering for the tastes of home, so an urgent request was sent back to his London office for Marmite and a few other store cupboard ingredients. Incredibly, these delights were sent out to Elton via the British Embassy's 'diplomatic bag', taking it outside the jurisdiction of customs officials, and ensuring its speedy delivery to the craving popstar. It was this same diplomatic bag that kept Winston Churchill in Cuban cigars during World War Two, courtesy of a well-wishing American.

Haddock and Artichoke Chowder with Parsnip Crisps

SERVES 6

25g unsalted butter
1 small onion, finely chopped
400g Jerusalem artichokes,
  roughly chopped
700ml good fish stock
 (or fish bouillon and water)
1 teaspoon Marmite
200g natural smoked haddock,
  skinned and flaked
75ml double cream
Cayenne pepper
Vegetable oil for deep-frying
1 large parsnip
Handful flat leaf parsley, chopped

It is best to use double cream rather than single as it won't split when over-heated.

1 Melt the butter and cook three quarters of the onion and half of the artichokes gently for 5 minutes in a covered saucepan making sure they don't brown. Add the fish stock and Marmite, bring to the boil and cover and simmer for about 15 minutes, until the vegetables are tender.

2 Begin to heat the vegetable oil ready for deep-frying the parsnip crisps. You should be able to make a sufficiently deep well of oil using a wok.

3 Cool the mixture a little and then blitz in a liquidiser until puréed. Return the soup to a clean pan and add the remaining vegetables. Simmer gently for about 10 minutes until the vegetables are tender, then add the fish, cream and cayenne pepper, stirring gently for about 5 minutes.

4 When the chowder is nearly ready, peel the parsnip. Once peeled, continue to use the potato peeler to cut full-length shavings off the parsnip and deep-fry in oil pre-heated to 190°c for about a minute until golden and crispy (like home-made crisps). Keep your eye on them as they will brown very quickly. Serve the soup strewn with the parsnip crisps and flat-leaf parsley.

Creamy Garlic Mushrooms on Toasted Brioche

SERVES 2

200g chestnut mushrooms
25g unsalted butter
1 clove garlic, crushed
100g crème fraîche
2 teaspoons Marmite
2 medium brioche rolls
1 dessertspoon chopped parsley

1 Wipe the mushrooms with a clean damp cloth and then cut each one into quarters. Melt the butter in a frying pan and add the garlic and mushrooms and sauté them until just cooked. Season generously with fresh black pepper and add the crème fraîche and the Marmite. Cook on a medium heat, stirring well, until the sauce has thickened to coat the mushrooms.

2 Split and toast the cut sides of the brioche rolls and place them on 2 warmed plates. Pile the creamy mushrooms over the brioche and garnish with a drift of parsley.

VITAMIN-RICH

Early into the twentieth century, people cottoned onto the fact that Marmite was rich in vitamins. Yeast extract was found to be packed with the vitamin B complex and Marmite retained these vitamins in a highly concentrated form. The spread began to find its way into households, hospitals and schools as a valuable addition to the diet.

Prawn and Marmite Sesame Toasts

SERVES 4

100g cooked peeled prawns
1 teaspoon cornflour
1 egg white, lightly beaten
4 slices white bread
Marmite for spreading
2 tablespoons sesame seeds
2 tablespoons vegetable oil

1 Finely mince the prawns to form a paste (a pestle and mortar will do the trick) and then add the cornflour and egg white to bind the mixture. Take the bread slices, cut off the crusts and spread with a thin layer of Marmite and then the minced prawns. Put the sesame seeds on a flat plate then press the bread slices, prawn side down, onto the sesame seeds until thickly coated.

2 Heat half the oil and gently fry each slice, prawn side down first, for 2-3 minutes, turning after 1-1½ minutes, until just golden. Add a little more oil as needed and cook the remaining slices in the same way. Serve while still warm, cut into triangles for an ideal munchie or a scummy starter.

Back in the '30s, following the discovery that yeast extract was enriched with so many vitamins, GOOD became the buzz word, and GOOD could be found in both the spread and the newly launched stock cubes.

Toasted Rye Bread with Goat's Cheese and Rocket

1 Cut and toast four slices of rye bread. The bread needs to be about 1cm thick.

2 While this is toasting, chop up the sunblush tomatoes, setting aside some of their delicious oil. Spread a teaspoon of Marmite on each piece of toast. Then lay enough slices of goat's cheese on top of the Marmite to cover the toast. Return the toast to the grill until the cheese just starts to melt.

 3 Sprinkle the sunblush tomatoes over the goat's cheese and finally add a flourish of rocket leaves over the top. Season generously with pepper and drizzle a little of the remaining oil from the tomatoes over the top.

SERVES 4

1 German country-style Rye bread (Landbrot)
50g sunblush tomatoes
Marmite
100g goat's cheese
Small bunch of rocket
Freshly milled black pepper

Pasta al Penne

SERVES 4

200g pasta al penne
1 tablespoon olive oil
100g dried wild mushrooms,
    pre-soaked in water for 30
    minutes and drained
1 teaspoon Marmite
150ml double cream
Black pepper
1 tablespoon of pitted black
    olives, roughly chopped
Freshly grated vintage Parmesan
Fresh parsley, chopped

1 Boil the pasta in plenty of salted water for about 8-10 minutes or until it is just *al dente*. While the pasta is cooking heat the olive oil in a frying pan and gently sauté the mushrooms for a couple of minutes. Add the Marmite to the mushrooms and toss them until well coated and then add the cream and some fresh pepper. Toss the mushrooms in the sauce for 2-3 minutes until the cream reduces down just a little and add the black olives.

2 Drain the cooked pasta and divide it between two warmed plates, then pile the mushrooms and sauce over the pasta. Finish with a good sprinkling of Parmesan and chopped parsley.

Manhattan Bagel

SERVES 1

1 bagel
Butter for spreading
Marmite for spreading
Good dollop of peanut butter
50g sliced pastrami
Handful of rocket leaves

1 Split and toast the cut sides of the bagel. Spread with a little butter and then a good layer of Marmite.

2 Next add the peanut butter, then the pastrami and finally pack the rocket on top and replace the lid of the bagel. Ready to go!

SUPERHERO

Self-declared, but a superhero nonetheless. Marmite Man has an online home where his story goes something like this: mild-mannered schoolboy, Yeast Extract, was deposited into a vat of toxic Marmite after a rough exchange following victory in a conkers match. [His] legend has it that in that vat he remained, for some fifteen years. When he finally emerged from the Marmite, Yeast realised he had special powers; namely an ability to shoot Marmite from his hands to long distances and a capacity to smell of Marmite. Hardly the résumé of a super-powered crime-fighter, perhaps. Mind you, this vigilante has also found time to focus his powers towards other areas, most notably an adaptation of the classic Pac-man game, with a neat twist! Visit his world at www.marmiteman.co.uk.

Chicken Club Sandwich

MAKES 2 SANDWICHES

6 rashers of rindless back bacon
3 large free-range eggs
Knob of butter for frying
6 slices good brown bread,
   toasted
3 dessertspoons mayonnaise
6 large Iceberg or Webb's lettuce
   leaves
1 chicken breast fillet,
   cooked and thinly sliced
2 tomatoes, sliced
Freshly ground black pepper
Marmite for spreading
Crisps or chips to serve (optional)

1 Prepare the fillings first. Grill the bacon until crispy. Whisk the eggs and then lightly scramble them in a knob of butter until just set.

2 Build each sandwich in this order. Lay a piece of toast on a chopping board, spread with mayonnaise, then cover it with a layer of lettuce leaves and half the sliced chicken breast. Cover this with a layer of sliced tomato and season with freshly milled black pepper. Take another piece of toast and spread with Marmite and put it Marmite side down on the tomatoes.

Spread the top side of the same piece of toast with Marmite, pour half the scrambled egg over this piece of toast and then cover it with half the crispy bacon rashers. Finish with another layer of lettuce leaves and the final piece of toast, spread with mayonnaise.

3 Secure each half of the sandwich with a cocktail stick and slice the sandwich diagonally. Serve while still warm for a delicious brunch with a few potato chips or home-made crisps.

Potato Wedges with Minted Yogurt Dip

SERVES 2

2 large baking potatoes, washed
2 level teaspoons Marmite
2 tablespoons olive oil
Small tub of Greek yogurt
2 teaspoons ready-made mint jelly

1 Put the potatoes in their skins into a large pan of water and boil gently for about 20 minutes until the potatoes are 'half cooked'. Drain the potatoes and allow to cool sufficiently to handle.

2 Pre-heat the oven to medium hot 375°F/190°C/ Gas 6. Whisk together the Marmite and olive oil. Cut each potato in half lengthways and then still working lengthways cut the potato into wedges about 2cm thick at the skin edge. Lay the wedges on a baking tray and douse each one with plenty of the Marmite oil. Roast in the oven for about 20 minutes until crispy and golden.

3 In a small dish mix together the yogurt and mint jelly, place it in the centre of a large plate and serve the golden wedges fanned all around the dip.

LOVE

RITA VOLEMIME
St Albans, Hertfordshire
'I keep a jar at work and one next to the bed that I slip my finger into when I'm peckish.'

Spinach, Marmite and Mozzarella Muffins

SERVES 1

1 English muffin
Butter for spreading
Marmite
2 tablespoons of wilted
  baby leaf spinach
50g Mozzarella, thinly sliced
Freshly milled black pepper
1 medium free-range egg

1 Pre-heat the grill to medium-high. Split and toast the muffins and spread each half with a little butter and then a good layer of Marmite. Pile the spinach onto each muffin half and top with the slices of Mozzarella. Season well with fresh black pepper.

2 Pop the stack back under the grill and cook for about 3-4 minutes or until the Mozzarella is just melting down the side. In the meantime poach the egg and serve the hot muffin topped with the poached egg.

SIMPLE IS BEST

Rigorous academic research has shown that the most pleasurable way to eat Marmite is thus:
a) use white bread (toasted to avoid dampness);
b) butter whilst still warm;
c) apply Marmite thinly, and leave small gaps;
d) cram it in your mouth as quickly as possible. What could be easier?

Marmite Popovers with Turkey and Tomato

MAKES 18 POPOVERS

2 large free-range eggs,
   plus one egg yolk
250ml milk
   (or milk and water mixed)
2 teaspoons Marmite
1 tablespoon melted butter
125g self-raising flour
Vegetable oil for greasing

TO SERVE
36 cherry tomatoes
   (2 per popover)
18 Turkey rashers (1 rasher per
   popover, each cut into 4 pieces)

Once made and cooled you can freeze the popovers for another day. Turkey rashers are available from most supermarkets and make a fun alternative to bacon.

1 Heat the oven to 230°C/450°F/Gas 8. In a large bowl beat the whole eggs plus the one egg yolk, then blend in the milk, Marmite and melted butter. Now sift in the flour and beat well until you have a creamy smooth consistency. Strain the mixture into a jug, then chill in the refrigerator for 10 minutes or until required. Batter is always better when made a little in advance.

2 Meanwhile lightly oil a 12-bun tray and place in the oven for 2-3 minutes to heat the oil. Remove from the oven and three-quarter-fill the hollows of the tin with the batter mixture – a bit like making Yorkshire puddings.

3 Bake in the oven for 15 minutes, then reduce the oven temperature to 200°C/400°F/Gas 6 and bake the popovers for a further 15 minutes until well risen and crisp. Avoid opening the oven door until cooked because the change in temperature may cause them to sink – and that would be a real shame. Serve the popovers piled with grilled cherry tomatoes and crispy turkey rashers.

Sicilian Scramble

SERVES 4

2 slices of focaccia bread
   (garlic and rosemary focaccia
   is sensational)
1 teaspoon Marmite
2 large slices of Prosciutto ham
   (enough to cover the bread)
Butter for scrambling
1 small green chilli, finely diced
4 free-range eggs
Celery salt
Freshly milled black pepper
Dash of Tabasco Sauce
1 tablespoon chopped
   sunblush tomatoes
Chopped fresh parsley

1 Lightly toast the focaccia bread and then spread with the Marmite. Lay the slices of ham on the hot Marmite toast.

2 Melt a little butter in a pan. Add the chilli, whisked eggs and season with the celery salt and pepper and then add a dash of Tabasco Sauce to taste. When the eggs are just beginning to set, add in the sunblush tomatoes and stir well.

3 Pile the scrambled eggs on top of the toast, garnish with fresh parsley and serve immediately.

Cream Cheese, Pistachio and Watercress Crumpets

1 Toast and butter the crumpets. Spread the Marmite on next, according to taste, and then the cream cheese.

2 Sprinkle the chopped pistachios over the top and finally pile on some good sprigs of watercress. The combination of the 'salty' Marmite, creamy cheese and peppery watercress is divine – hence two per person!

SERVES 2

4 crumpets
Unsalted butter
Marmite for spreading
75g cream cheese
50g chopped pistachio nuts
A bunch of watercress`

HATE

MARTIE THAME
London
'When I was young, my older brother told me it was chocolate spread. I've not forgiven him to this day.'

Panini with Marmite Tapenade, Taleggio and Sweet Peppers

SERVES 4

1 red pepper, deseeded
2 tablespoons olive oil
Pinch sugar
225g black olives, stoned
1 teaspoon Marmite
25g capers, drained
1 teaspoon lemon juice
Freshly ground black pepper
1 dessertspoon breadcrumbs
   (optional)
1 small ciabatta loaf
50g Taleggio cheese
   (or similar Italian hard cheese)
Few basil leaves, torn

1 Set the grill to medium-high. Cut the pepper in half and brush with a little olive oil, add a pinch of sugar, and grill skin side up until charred. Remove the peppers leaving the grill on. Put the seared peppers in a plastic bag and leave to cool – this will help lift the skin from the flesh easily.

2 In the meantime make the tapenade by blitzing the olives, Marmite and capers in a food processor until you have a purée. Then gradually add the olive oil followed by the lemon juice and pepper. If at this stage the tapenade is not like a firm paste, mix in a dessertspoon of breadcrumbs. This tapenade will keep for a week in the fridge, so if you have some left over keep it ready for your next feast.

3 Cut the ciabatta in half lengthways, toast and then spread with the tapenade, followed by the roughly chopped peppers. Using a potato peeler cut shavings off the Taleggio and sprinkle over the peppers. Serve at once with the torn basil leaves scattered on top.

Marmite celebrated its centenary year in style. 2002 saw a frenzy of activity around Marmite – commemorative jars, limited-edition designer T-shirts, brightly branded London taxis, and a trio of memorable TV adverts.

And one of those adverts, of course, featured Zippy. He revealed his dislike to a shocked nation by zipping up and taking cover under the table!

Marmite Island Dip

SERVES 3

150g Philadelphia Lite
1 teaspoon Marmite
1 teaspoon finely chopped
   coriander leaves
Tabasco Sauce
6 small gherkins
   (4 chopped, 2 for garnish)
2 teaspoons tomato puree
Mixed salad leaves for garnish
Breadsticks or tortillas for dipping

1 In a bowl mix together the Philadelphia cheese, Marmite, coriander, a couple of drops of Tabasco Sauce, chopped gherkins and tomato purée until they are blended into a thick textured dip.

2 Spoon the cheesy mixture into a suitable dipping bowl and scatter a few salad leaves around the base. Take the remaining 2 gherkins and make 4 cuts lengthways, without cutting all the way through, and open the gherkins up to form fans. Arrange these on top of the dip and serve with tumblers of breadsticks and a scattering of tortillas or a selection of fresh crudités.

Marmite Corn Fritters

SERVES 4

1 egg
2 level tablespoons
  self-raising flour
1/4 teaspoon Cayenne pepper
1/2 teaspoon Worcestershire
  sauce
1 teaspoon Marmite
326g tin of sweetcorn, drained
Vegetable oil for frying
Bacon and maple syrup,
  to accompany

1 Make a stiff batter by mixing together the beaten egg, sieved flour and Cayenne pepper. Beat well and then add the Worcestershire sauce and Marmite and beat for a further minute. Fold in the sweetcorn so that it is well mixed with the batter and refrigerate for 20 minutes.

2 Oil a griddle or heavy frying pan over a medium-high heat and spoon on tablespoons of the mixture. Cook for 4-5 minutes, turning once, until golden brown. Kids love this dish, which is great served with grilled bacon and maple syrup.

OLD TIMER

Among the younger kids on the block:

Teabags (invented by Thomas Sullivan, 1904)
The cornflake (invented by William Kellog, 1906)
Plastic (discovered 1907)
Crossword puzzle (first published New York, 1912)

Traffic lights (first installed outside the British House of Commons, 1914)
Zip fasteners (invented 1914)
The band-aid bandage (launched by Johnson & Johnson, 1921)
London red double-decker bus (1925)
McDonalds (founded 1959)

Devilled Kidneys

SERVES 3-4

2 teaspoons Worcestershire
  sauce
1 teaspoon Marmite
1 tablespoon tomato purée
1 tablespoon lemon juice
1 tablespoon French mustard
Good pinch cayenne pepper
8 lambs' kidneys
1/2 teaspoon fennel seeds
25g unsalted butter
Freshly ground black pepper
Chopped fresh parsley

1 You can easily up the heat of this traditional dish by adding more cayenne or by replacing the French mustard with English mustard.

2 Mix together the Worcestershire sauce, Marmite, tomato purée, lemon juice, French mustard and cayenne pepper in a small bowl.

3 Cut each kidney into 3. Melt the butter in a frying pan and when sizzling slide in the kidneys. Toss the kidneys and fennel seeds in the butter for 3-4 minutes, season with black pepper and then add the spicy mixture. Keep tossing the whole dish for about another minute until the kidneys are coated in the rich sauce. Kidneys cook quickly; when ready they will still have a hint of pink in the centre. Serve with good basmati rice or thick toasted triangles and scatter the finished dish with chopped parsley.

Another of Marmite's centenary-commissioned TV adverts. This time, the unveiling of the freak called 'Marmite Man'. Audiences gasped as he spooned the notorious spread straight from the jar into his mouth!

Pancetta and Gruyère Frittata

SERVES 3-4

250g diced pancetta
1 medium red chilli,
   de-seeded and finely chopped
6 large free-range eggs
150g Gruyère cheese,
   roughly grated
1 level teaspoon Marmite
1 teaspoon fresh chives,
   finely chopped
Freshly ground black pepper
1 tablespoon flat-leaf parsley,
   roughly chopped

1 Cook the Pancetta in it's own fat for 5 minutes over a medium heat until lightly browned. Add the chilli and cook for 30 seconds.

2 Beat the eggs lightly in a large jug and mix in the grated cheese, Marmite and chopped chives. Season lightly with pepper.

3 Pre-heat the grill to it's highest setting. Pour the egg mixture into the frying pan and cook over a low heat for 5-8 minutes or until the egg has set. Put the pan under the grill about 10cm from the heat. Let it cook for a few minutes or until golden on top – but do keep an eye on it. Sprinkle the parsley over, cut into thick wedges and serve.

You will need a non-stick frying pan, 30cm in diameter and about 5cm deep.

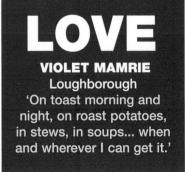

LOVE
VIOLET MAMRIE
Loughborough
'On toast morning and night, on roast potatoes, in stews, in soups... when and wherever I can get it.'

Basil French Toast with Dolcelatte and Pimento

SERVES 2

3 medium free-range eggs
100ml milk
Level tablespoon of freshly
  chopped basil leaves
Freshly ground black pepper
Marmite for spreading
4 slices firm rustic bread
150g Dolcelatte, cut into 4 slices
1-2 large red peppers, sliced
2 tablespoons olive oil

1 In a shallow bowl mix together the egg, milk, chopped basil and pepper. Spread the bread with Marmite and dip each slice into the mixture until well soaked and transfer to a large plate. Add the Dolcelatte and the slices of pepper. Season well with fresh pepper and then sandwich together the remaining slices of bread, gently pressing together to seal them.

2 Heat half the olive oil on a griddle or in a large non-stick frying pan and fry the sandwiches over a low heat for about 3-4 minutes on each side until golden, adding the remaining oil as needed. Check that the bread has cooked through and is not soggy inside and then drain on kitchen paper to remove any excess oil. Serve immediately on warmed plates.

Red Onion Marmalade and Goat's Cheese Tartlet

SERVES 4

1 pack puff pastry
Flour for dusting
Marmite
4 dessertspoons red onion
   marmalade (available from
   most good food stores)
150g soft goat's cheese
1 medium egg yolk plus 1
   tablespoon water beaten
   together
Few sprigs of freshly torn
   flat-leaf parsley
Black pepper

1 Pre-heat the oven to 200°C/
400°F/Gas 6. Roll the pastry
out on a lightly floured board
to form a large square and
then cut the pastry into
8 smaller squares about
8-10cm square.

2 Spread a layer of Marmite
over each square and
then turn up the edges
to make a border.
Now add a tablespoon of
onion marmalade to each
tartlet, spreading it evenly
with the back of a spoon.
Add a slice of goat's
cheese on top and put
the tartlets onto a floured
baking tray.

3 Brush the borders of the
tartlets with the egg and
water wash and chill for
at least 15 minutes before
baking in the centre of the
oven for 15 minutes.

4 Allow the finished tartlets
to cool a little and serve
strewn with the torn parsley
leaves and some fresh
black pepper.

**Puff pastry rises better when
cold from the refrigerator,
so make these tartlets in
advance and cook when
ready.**

*Anarchy on the roads.
Billboards and bus posters
spelt out the bitter truth.*

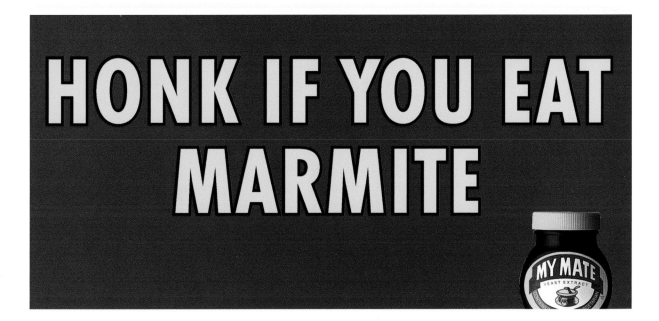

Linguine with Bacon and Egg

SERVES 4

200g linguine (thin spaghetti)
1dessertspoon Marmite
Drizzle of olive oil
4 medium free-range eggs
8 rashers of streaky bacon
2 tbsp freshly chopped parsley
Fresh black pepper
Parmesan shavings

It's worth getting a wooden spaghetti spoon to make stirring and serving much easier.

1 Cook the linguine in plenty of unsalted boiling water for 8-10 minutes or until just *al dente*. Drain the pasta and add the Marmite and olive oil, give it a good stir and leave aside covered to keep warm and for the linguine to absorb the flavourings. Whilst this is happening, grill the bacon until crispy and fry the eggs quite quickly in a little olive oil. This is a dish where a crispy base to the egg looks and tastes really good.

2 Dice the bacon and add to the linguine, together with most of the chopped parsley and some freshly milled black pepper. Pile the pasta into warm serving bowls, top with the crispy fried eggs, the remaining fresh parsley and the Parmesan shavings.

FIGHTING FIT

The word vitamin was only coined in 1912, to define chemicals that were found to be necessary in our diets. Marmite was packed with B vitamins... and still is.

MARMITE
for Family Fitness

CONTAINS THE VALUABLE B2 VITAMINS

FAMILY SIZES	
8 oz - 4'6	1 oz - 10ᵈ
16 oz - 8'-	2 oz - 1'6
	4 oz - 2'9

Mushroom, Ham and Honey Stack

SERVES 4

FOR THE PANCAKES
280g plain flour
1 teaspoon salt
2 teaspoons baking powder
2 tablespoons caster sugar
225ml milk
1 teaspoon Marmite
3 free-range eggs, beaten
50g melted unsalted butter

FOR THE TOPPING
200g button mushrooms
1 tablespoon olive oil
100g diced smoked ham
Runny chestnut honey
   for pouring

1 Sift the flour, salt, baking powder and sugar into a bowl, then whisk in the milk, Marmite, beaten eggs and butter mixing to form a thick batter. If it isn't very smooth don't worry and don't be tempted to over-mix.

2 Heat a lightly buttered griddle or frying pan and add 2 tablespoons of the batter for each pancake, cooking in batches of 3-4 at a time. As soon as you see bubbles forming on the surface of the pancakes flip them over. They will need about a minute on each side. Keep the pancakes warm while you repeat, using up all the mixture.

3 Slice $^3/_4$ of the mushrooms, leaving a few whole for topping the stacks. Heat the olive oil in a pan and sauté the whole ones first adding the sliced ones later until they are just golden. Toss in the diced ham and cook with the mushrooms for no more than a minute. For each serving, layer some sliced mushrooms and ham between four pancakes in a stack on a warmed plate and then some whole mushrooms on the top. Finish with a good drizzle of chestnut honey.

Roasted Onion Soup with Cheddar Croûtons

SERVES 4-6

4 medium onions
40g unsalted butter
Sea salt and fresh black pepper
1 dessertspoon Demerara sugar
175ml of dry white wine
1.5 litres good vegetable stock
1 teaspoon Marmite
1 small French stick
100g grated Cheddar
Fresh thyme

1 Peel the onions and quarter them from the top to the bottom. Lay them on a roasting tray and scatter them with pieces of the butter. Season with a little salt and lots of black pepper. Roast for about 30-40 minutes until they begin to darken.

2 Allow the onion quarters to cool a little and then slice them into half moons. Put them in a large heavy based saucepan, add the sugar and wine and bring to the boil, bubbling until the wine has almost disappeared. Add the stock and Marmite, bring back to the boil and then cook gently for about 20 minutes.

3 To make the croûtons, slice the French bread to allow 2 per person and toast on one side under the grill. Turn them over and sprinkle with a little grated cheese and return to the grill long enough to melt the cheese. Serve the hot soup with the melted cheese croûtons floating temptingly on the surface and scattered with fresh thyme.

Marmite's 2003 'Lifeguard' advert. There's no resuscitative kiss quite like the one that comes immediately after a Marmite-sarnie lunch!

Roasted Vegetable Filo Parcels

SERVES 2

Ready-made filo pastry
1 small aubergine
1 small courgette
1/2 red pepper, deseeded
4 shallots, peeled
2 tablespoons olive oil
1 teaspoon Marmite
1 teaspoon white sugar
Melted butter
50g Philadelphia Lite
Bunch watercress

1 Heat the oven to 375°F/190°C/Gas 6. Cut the different vegetables into 2-3cm dice and put them onto a baking tray. Mix the olive oil with the Marmite and drizzle it over the cut vegetables, tossing them to make sure they are well coated. Sprinkle with the sugar and roast for about 20 minutes until still crunchy but seared around the edges. Remove from the oven and leave to cool just a little.

2 Cut the filo pastry sheet into 20cm squares. Brush with melted butter and lay one square on top of another each time rotating 15 degrees to form a star shape with 3 squares of filo. (Easy to think of the degrees as 5, 10, 15 minutes past the hour and so on).

Put a teaspoon of cream cheese in the centre of each star plus a tablespoon of mixed vegetables. Gather up the outer points of the pastry star, pinch together and twist at the neck to form a little parcel. Repeat with the remaining cream cheese and vegetables to make four parcels (you will have vegetables left over). Put all of the parcels on a greased baking sheet, brush them all over with melted butter and cook in the centre of a medium oven 350°F/180°C/Gas 5 for 5-8 minutes until the pastry turns golden brown at the edges.

3 Allow the parcels to cool a little and serve with any remaining vegetables around the base of the parcels and a big bunch of fresh peppery watercress.

The Marmite Steam Train

SERVES 1

2 slices white bread
Butter for spreading
Marmite
2 slices tomato or cucumber
4 teaspoons cream cheese

Perfect for kids of all ages!

1 Toast the bread and spread with butter and then with Marmite. Trim the crusts off the toast and cut each slice into 9 equal squares.

2 On a large plate assemble the train out of the squares. Start with a row of 6 along the bottom of the plate. Working upwards, lay another row of 6 squares.

3 Next add 2 squares at the left hand side, leave a gap and add 1 square for the stack. Leave another gap and add 2 squares for the cab and in the final top right hand corner 1 square for the roof of the cab.

4 Place the 2 slices of tomato or cucumber at the bottom to form 2 wheels at the side of the train. For the final touch add the cream cheese in 4 separate spoonfuls to form puffs of smoke coming out of the stack.

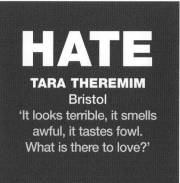

HATE
TARA THEREMIM
Bristol
'It looks terrible, it smells awful, it tastes fowl. What is there to love?'

Marmite
Alternative uses!

Marmite
A 'potted' history

Alternative uses!

One

Turn the front room of your house into your very own forensic laboratory. Prepare a tray of thinly-applied Marmite spread and a pad of white paper. Invite several mischievous friends round. Greet them at the door with a terribly suspicious look. Request each of them to place their ten digits into the tray of Marmite Spread, then have them press their mucky fingers onto the paper. Suggest that they could be in trouble, and that they will soon be hearing from you. Wave each of them away.

Two

Dip tiny hand-rolled pellets of blu-tack into a pot of Marmite spread, then cut neat holes into the pockets of an old pair of trousers. Take a clutch of pellets into hand and place hand into pocket before visiting the house of a rabbit-keeping friend. Upon entering the house, pace around as many square metres of carpet as you can, slowly releasing brown pellets from your clenched hand as you walk. Once decanted in full, look to the floor and feign horror at the sloppy domestic standards set by your friend.

Three

Fool your meat-eating friends! Steam the wrappers off Bovril jars, dry them out and then glue them onto jars of Marmite spread. Remove the yellow lid and paint vermillion red. Re-seal when dry. Create a small 'den' in some nook of the kitchen and wait to see the looks of surprise/delight/disgust on the faces of your ignorant friends!

Four

Brighten up dull Formica kitchen surfaces by dipping a rag liberally into a jar of Marmite spread and dragging across any worktop areas in need of sprucing up*. Aim for an authentic 'woodgrain' effect, (but don't worry if your efforts do not even get close: it will look better). Allow several weeks to dry before finishing with two to three topcoats of clear varnish.

* Sugar-soap surfaces first.

Five

Take four single bed sheets and three 500g-jars of Marmite spread. Paste liberally over all of the sheets. Nail the coated sheets to the ceiling above your bed. You now have a 'protective net' which should attract (but prove impenetrable) to insects and small animals of all forms. Courting individuals should beware possible side-effects that may deter partner from bedroom vicinity.

A 'potted' history

	Marmite world	**Outside world**
1866	A German chemist by the name of Justin Liebig discovered that the waste of brewers' yeast in the beer brewing process could be made into a concentrate that resulted in a protein-rich paste with a meaty flavour.	On 27 March 1866, Andrew Rankin patented his design for the urinal, much to the relief of generations of men to follow. He could not have foreseen its transmutation into modern art object some fifty years later.
1902	The Marmite Food Extract Company Limited started life as a public company on June 13th. Having negotiated the acquisition of the patents for health-giving yeast extract, the directors set up a small factory in Burton-on-Trent, centre of the British brewing industry where the all-important yeast was readily available.	Morris Michtom took heart from a cartoon that showed US President Theodore Roosevelt refusing to shoot a bear cub. Inspired, Michtom began to sell button-eyed bears made by his wife, Rose. With the President's consent, Michtom named his creation 'Teddy' bears, and went on to establish one of America's largest doll and toy factories.
1905	A small sales force was set up and in the report of the Board to the Shareholders a dividend of 6% was recommended.	

Marmite world

Outside world

1907

A new Marmite factory opened at Camberwell Green in London to meet the needs of a growing market.

In 1908, John Krohn set off on a walk that would cover the entire perimeter of America. Ambitious enough, you might think. Well, Krohn decided to take his wheelbarrow for company. Krohn and his one-wheeled friend covered more than 9,000 miles, completing the walk in 351 days, an average of just more than 25 miles a day. Krohn managed to get through 11 pairs of shoes and 112 pairs of socks, and the wheelbarrow required four replacement wheels.

1912

The word vitamin was created to describe chemicals necessary to diets. This was a major boost to Marmite when it was realised that yeast provided a good source of five types of B vitamin. This resulted in quantities of Marmite flooding into schools, hospitals and other public institutions.

1924

Marmite Limited became a wholly owned subsidiary of Bovril Limited.

1927

With lack of space for expansion at Camberwell Green, Marmite production was moved to a disused brewery at Vauxhall, London.

	Marmite world	**Outside world**
1928	A change to the pot! This was the year that first saw a change to the earthenware pot. The 25-year-old pot was changed to a glass jar with a metal lid, setting in place the traditional style of jar that has barely changed to the present day.	Bingo was officially established on 3 December 1929 by American toy salesman Edwin S. Lowe, who took a game called 'Beano' to New York. Upon completing her card, one of Lowe's friends erred with a shout of 'Bingo' and an institution was born!
1930	Marmite stock cubes were launched in a distinctive green tin and were easy to crumble straight into stews and soups. They were eventually dropped to concentrate on production of Marmite spread and were re-launched again 65 years later.	A significant side-development in the history of Marmite: Wonder Bread – the world's first loaf of sliced bread! Sliced bread revolutionised sandwich-making, so much so that it gave rise to the famous saying, 'the best thing since sliced bread'.
1935	Marmite recipes featured in the book *Invalid Dishes,* hailing the wonder of Marmite.	Charles B. Darrow sold his invented game to Parker Brothers. Monopoly became America's bestselling game, and Darrow became a multi-millionaire.
1956	Marmite sponsored the British team in the Olympic Games in Melbourne.	On 12 December 1954, the first instance of a meteorite striking a human being was recorded. It occurred in Alabama. It was said to have smashed through the roof of the house of Mrs Elizabeth Hodges, tearing through

Marmite world	Outside world
	into the living room, where it bounced off a radio and finally struck the recumbent Mrs Hodges on the hip. The rock weighed $8^1/_2$ pounds and was 7 inches long. Mrs Hodges spent five days in hospital with her bruised hip.

1969

A new brighter label was introduced for all pack sizes.

1968 marked the first appearance of the 'F-word' in a movie. It was enunciated by Marianne Faithfull in the film *I'll Never Forget Whatshisname*. 16 years later, Brian De Palma's 1984 movie, *Scarface* would feature the word more than 200 times – virtually every 30 seconds.

1970

Bovril Limited (who owned Marmite) was acquired by Sir James Goldsmith's Cavenham Foods Limited. Later, Beechams, who later became SmithKline Beecham, bought the brand.

1973

Marmite was being advertised as the 'Growing Up Spread'.

1974

This year brought a shortage of the traditional glass jar. There was a brief, but worrying, interlude in which Marmite was sold in more conventionally shaped jars.

	Marmite world	**Outside world**
1980	The My Mate Marmite campaign began: 'My Mate, Whose Mate? My Mate, Marmite'.	St Winifred's School Choir top the Xmas chart with 'There's No One Quite Like Grandma'.
1984	The first yellow plastic lid.	The famous emergency hotline that linked the White House to the Kremlin wasn't established until 1984. Prior to this date, the only direct link to the Kremlin had been via an awkward teleprinter link that churned out text messages that then needed translating.
1990	CPC (UK) Limited acquired both Bovril and Marmite brands.	
1995	Marmite stock cubes relaunched.	
1996	The 'Love-it, Hate-it' campaign begins.	
1998	CPC (UK) Limited changed its name to Bestfoods Inc.	
2000	Unilever PLC purchased Bestfoods and Marmite became a Unilever Bestfoods brand. 'Marmite Mania' was launched. The Cheese and Marmite savoury spread was available in 150g tubs.	The most overhyped year in history. The world divided: some thought the ground would open and swallow us up (the 'Doomsday' camp); others sat and waited for their computers to implode, the lights to flicker, the National Grid to malfunction, and man to be returned to his Neanderthal roots / primordial soup (the 'Millennium Bug' camp). Both transpired to be nothing more than damp squibs.

2002

Marmite world

Marmite's centenary year.

Having remained largely unchanged since 1902, Marmite now ventured into brand extension. It teamed up with Walkers Crisps to produce Marmite-flavoured crisps. Children's TV favourite Zippy arrived on TV screens only to be rendered speechless by a Marmite soldier.
33 London taxis were painted with the Marmite slogan Love it or Hate it and HRH the Duke of Edinburgh visited the Marmite factory during a Golden Jubilee visit to Burton-on-Trent.
A series of limited-edition commemorative jars were launched, including the original 1902 jar design as well as those from 1940 and 1970.
Fashion designer Vivienne Westwood helped celebrate the centenary by designing an exclusive limited edition T-shirt.

Outside world

Millionaire Mark Shuttleworth became the first African citizen in space and only the second paying guest ever to go into orbit. Shuttleworth stayed at the International Space Station for ten days. He made his money with an internet security business which he started in his parents' garage and then sold four years later for $500m. Shuttleworth's ticket was said to have cost around $20m. He underwent extensive training and also learned Russian in order to better-communicate with his flight colleagues. Just prior to his return to Earth, the following e-mail missive was found to be performing an orbit of its own across the personal computers of Earth-dwelling humorists:

'When Mark Shuttleworth (rich space tourist) returns from outer space, everyone dress up in ape suits. Pass it on.'

Author's acknowledgments

To my wife Lynda who has shared the whole experience and who added her culinary expertise to my creativity. Thank you for being my Marmiteeny, xx. To Clare Barrett BSc for all her help with the nutritional comment. Thank you Clare for your enthusiasm and expertise in balancing these Marmite recipes. Thank you to Sarah Francis from the Whatley Grange Cookery School in Somerset who has helped to prevent me straying from the food technological path. Without Sarah this book would have missed the little extra to make it special. A big thank you to Oliver Bradley who was the Marmite Brand Manager and trusted us with this project – I said we wouldn't let you down.

Finally, my thanks to the publishing team at Absolute Press – Jon, Meg and Matt – whose understanding and encouragement were priceless. They have done an excellent job in assembling The Marmite Cookbook. Thank you so very much.

Publisher's thanks

Thanks to Unilever Best Foods UK Ltd – especially Oli, Susie and Sarah. Thanks to Freud Communications and the Robert Opie Collection. Thanks to John Dixon, Andy Langley, Meg Devenish and Doug Schneider for their editorial/pictorial contributions and suggestions, and to Russell Tuck for photographing his arm at the eleventh hour. Thanks to Rachel and Heidi at John Brown, and to Caroline at Kobal.